THE WEARY WORLD STILL REJOICES

Amanda Geidl

ISBN-13: 9798753167583
ISBN-10: 1477123456

Cover design by: Kate Ranstrom
Library of Congress Control Number: 2018675309

Printed in the United States of America

For Dave, my always and forever favorite human.

CONTENTS

INTRODUCTION

I began writing these devotionals in 2020, the year the world was rocked by Covid-19. I posted them on both Instagram and Facebook as an attempt to encourage those within my sphere. There seemed to be an abundance of worry and fear along with a yearning for the normalcy of celebrating Christmas. People put their Christmas trees up early, listened to Christmas music, bought all the twinkle lights, emptying the shelves at the stores, and tried to pretend that the world wasn't a mess for a couple of months. It was understandable; everyone had experienced suffering in one form or another.

I found I was feeling encouraged as I read the Christmas stories in Matthew and Luke and researched the prophecies that predicted the details concerning Jesus' coming. After the holidays ended, I removed my posts from social media in the event that I ever wanted to publish them. I began writing questions to accompany each reading as well. Finally, I set it aside and promptly moved on with my other writing.

I worked on various writing projects over the course of the next few months, and before I knew it, it was September. I pulled out the manuscript and realized that I had written all the questions for the devotional! I had completely forgotten I had finished writing them. I began to pray and ask God to show me if I really ought to move forward with this project or stop wasting my time.

The first weekend of October, my church had a women's event, Girl Time, and my girls and I went for the evening. My fellow small group member, Kate Ranstrom, was a vendor at the event, selling her prophetic prayer art. I didn't have any spending money and told her I was bummed; I really wanted to support her and buy her art.

"That's okay! I have a bunch of free stuff here," she said, pointing to a small pile of hand-painted harvest cards and various bookmarks.

One bookmark in particular caught my eye: a blue feather with fine brushstrokes. I picked it up and thanked her for it, but she stopped me.

"Turn it over," she said.

I turned it over, and in her script, I read these words,

A call to write for the Lord.

I was astounded. She knew I was writing several months prior to this evening, but how did she know

I was going to pick up that particular bookmark? There were several there on the table.

Tears began sliding down my cheeks, and I made my way to hug Kate. She explained how it happened.

"The Lord told me to paint that bookmark for you, and if you didn't pick it up, I was to give it to you. But you picked it up!"

What faith! The following Sunday, my pastor approached me between services and asked me if my devotional was something the church could use together. I told him I believed so.

I thanked God for the confirmation to keep writing, and I have been polishing this book for the last three weeks. I originally had hoped to publish this book through a traditional publisher, but I sensed this was an open door from the Lord to print this book for our church and anyone else who may like to use it to focus on Jesus' coming this December.

To my great joy, my friend, Kate, agreed to paint the cover of this book. I was giddy with excitement when she sent me her completed work. I loved each symbolic detail she included. Kate's art is available for purchase, and you can read more about her and where to find her online in the back of this book.

This book is full of messages of hope that point to Jesus. I truly believe He is the only one who can fill your deepest needs, calm your greatest fears, and deliver you from all sin. This is my Christmas gift to you —Jesus.

CHAPTER 1: HOLIDAYS IN THE DARK

December 1

Living in a land occupied by a foreign military wears on the souls of the conquered inhabitants. Looking over one's shoulder becomes a familiar practice. A father watches his hard-earned money slip through his hands in exorbitant taxes to this foreign invader, leaving little to provide for his family's sustenance. There's a cry in the broken hearts of the people, for divine deliverance, but God is seemingly silent. If God won't intervene, they thought, then perhaps we should take circumstances into our own hands and revolt! Zealot bands grew and plotted rebellion in Israel against their Roman overlords. It's no wonder that many were unaware that God had a different plan for the weary world.

God's quiet and humble mission was to send His Son as an infant, completely reliant upon His teenage mother and willing adoptive father. He didn't come with a sword in hand, on a white horse, ready to rout the enemy and set His people free. Instead, angelic fanfare announced His arrival to some shepherds on a starry night while He was being born of a virgin in a dwelling meant for livestock, not a newborn babe. This was a subversive mission, not to save Israel from their Roman occupiers, but to ultimately set all of humanity free from the sin that occupies our hearts.

The place we find ourselves is on the back side of the mission—He already came, but we often find that we can relate to those first century Jews who were living in fear and feeling trapped. We, too, have lived lives of revolt, averse to waiting for God to fulfill His promises to us. We've been so unwilling to wait for Him, we also resist His rule and good plans for us. Sometimes, we're just living in avoidance of doing the small things He wants us to do. We've all walked in the dark. It was this darkness, this refusal to walk by faith, this disobedience, that prompted the God of the universe to reach down and send His Son to be the Savior of the world, the Light in our darkness.

The people who walked in darkness
have seen a great light;
those who dwelt in a land of deep darkness,
on them has light shone (Isaiah 9:2, ESV).

God has brought us a permanent holiday (holy-day) where the weak are made strong, the foolish become wise, and ashes are exchanged for beauty. Every day is a holy-day when we see Jesus, the Holy One who gives His holiness for our sin, His life for our death, and His victory for our failure.

Instead of distracting ourselves from the difficulties of life, let's press in to hear Him. Instead of waiting for the temporary relief from disease, isolation, and bondage, let's turn to Jesus and find healing, belonging, and freedom.

For to us a child is born,
to us a son is given;
and the government shall be upon his shoulder,
and his name shall be called
Wonderful Counselor, Mighty God,
Everlasting Father, Prince of Peace (Isaiah 9:6, ESV).

* * *

Going Deeper

1. What are you resisting or avoiding this Christmas season? A relationship that needs repair? An assignment God has called you to do? Repentance of sin

that's entangling you? List them.

2. How does the light of Jesus' arrival shine into those dark places in your heart and life?

3. Write out a prayer here asking Jesus to shine His light in your darkness, and ask Him what steps you need to take to move toward holiness and healing in His name.

CHAPTER 2: INTERRUPTED

December 2

The young teenage girl, Mary, had most of her life ahead of her. She was engaged to be married to Joseph, and their wedding was soon approaching. Suddenly, an angel appeared, and all of her plans were instantly altered, interrupted.

The angel told her that she would give birth to a miraculous child by the Holy Spirit. She didn't understand how it could be possible, but she didn't pout or grumble about this sudden change of direction. She received the word of the Lord to carry Christ. Her response is humble, aware of her own lowliness and her position before an Almighty God.

> *Behold, I am the servant of the Lord; let it be to me according to your word (Luke 1:38, ESV).*

We live in a world turned upside down. Everything normal has come undone; upheaval and change have marked all of our stories. In the interruption, the change of direction, the upheaval, what would it look like for us to declare that we are the servants of the Lord, so let it be?

It may look like doing hard things without complaints, grieving our losses, taking the next step into the unknown, and holding out hope for ourselves and others. It might even look like laying aside our plans for the normal and comfortable and embracing discomfort and struggle.

The beauty of making Mary's words our own is that in doing so, we are making room for Jesus to show up, just as she did. We can't do this on our own or even for ourselves. We must lay our comfortable lives down in order to carry Christ and offer Him to a hurting world. He is the gift we give in suffering. He is the gift we give in loss. He is the gift we give in discomfort. We are the servants of the Lord. Let it be unto us according to Your word.

Going Deeper

1. What ways have you experienced interruption in

your own life?

2. Pray through each interruption, and declare to the Lord that you are His servant and you receive what He is offering you in these interruptions.

3. Write the name of someone you know who is in a hard transition or life interruption. Think of a practical way you can be an encouragement to them at this time, then schedule a time on your calendar to be intentional in ministering to them.

CHAPTER 3: WAITING IN FAITH

December 3

For Elizabeth, time was of the essence. She had waited. Years passed. Nothing. There were whispers; others wondered what she had done to deserve a barren womb and empty arms.

But throughout her waiting, Father God was eagerly waiting to grant her the gift of a son, John, literally translated, "The Gift of God." Perhaps knowing she would eventually have a son would have made the waiting time bearable, perhaps not. God's timing was everything.

It was essential that Elizabeth not give birth to John too early—he must be born at the right moment, just before the Messiah. Elizabeth was advanced in years, likely past the childbearing age. Her cousin, Mary, was a young teenager. This means when Elizabeth was first married, Mary hadn't even been born! Elizabeth had to wait. Wait for Mary to be born. Wait for Mary to come of age. Wait until it would be a miracle. Wait until the perfect moment.

We're all waiting. Holding our breath. Waiting for things to change. Waiting for a break in the clouds. Waiting for a miracle moment. Friend, God sees you just as He saw Elizabeth. His good purpose wasn't thwarted in her life, and it won't be thwarted in yours. May we say with Elizabeth who recognized the eye of God on her in her waiting,

> *"The Lord has done this for me," she said. "In these days he has shown his favor and taken away my disgrace among the people." (Luke 1:25, NIV).*

* * *

Going Deeper

1. What has you holding your breath this December? Finances? Illness? Fear? Relationships or lack thereof?

2. What would waiting on God look like in your situation? Is this a place of prayer? A place of surrender to His will? Is there an action step for you to take in faith?

3. How have you seen God work in your life before today? How has He provided? How has He surprised you? How has He helped you? List those gifts from Him, and then take a moment to thank Him for those gifts.

CHAPTER 4: GOD'S FAITHFULNESS IN THE JOURNEY

December 4

Joseph and Mary resided in Galilee, in the good-for-nothing town of Nazareth. Joseph had already had the dream from the Lord instructing him to take Mary as his wife. In faith, he married her and brought her home with him, but their marriage remained unconsummated (Matthew 1:20-25).

Caesar Augustus ruled Rome at the time, and he decreed a census be taken of his conquered territories. It was required that each family return to their ancestral town to be registered in this census. Joseph and Mary were both of the house of David, so it was imperative for them to return to Bethlehem.

It was a ninety mile trip. We're not told if Mary

rode a donkey or walked on foot. We're not told exactly how pregnant she was, but the roads to get from Nazareth to Bethlehem were fraught with wild animals, thieves, and numerous hills to climb. The trip probably took at least one week if not two.

When Caesar called this census, requiring this return to ancestral homes, he didn't realize that his decision would result in the fulfillment of a prophecy made by Micah seven hundred years prior.

But you, Bethlehem Ephrathah,
though you are small among the clans of Judah,
out of you will come for me
one who will be ruler over Israel,
whose origins are from of old,
from ancient times.
Therefore Israel will be abandoned
until the time when she who is in labor bears a son,
and the rest of his brothers return
to join the Israelites (Micah 5:2-3, NIV).

Jesus had to be born in Bethlehem. The chief priests and scribes confirmed this to King Herod when the wise men showed up looking for a newborn king. Interestingly enough, when Jesus was an adult, some were insisting He couldn't be the Messiah because He was from Galilee. How little they knew about Him! God's sovereignty and faithfulness to keep His promises plays out in the smallest details proving He is a God who keeps His word.

O little town of Bethlehem,
How still we see thee lie!
Above thy deep and dreamless sleep
The silent stars go by.
Yet in thy dark streets shineth
The everlasting light;
The hopes and fears of all the years
Are met in thee tonight.

FROM "O LITTLE TOWN OF BETHLEHEM" BY PHILLIPS BROOKS[1]

* * *

Going Deeper

1. In what ways have you seen God's faithfulness in the details of your own life?

2. Write a prayer of gratitude to God for His faithfulness.

3. What details in life right now are causing you fear and anxiety? Offer them up to Him now in faith, knowing He will work them out for your good (Romans 8:28; Philippians 4:6-7).

CHAPTER 5: THE SMALLNESS OF THE SAVIOR

December 5

Too small and insignificant to even be counted among the clans of Judah, this was Bethlehem. Yet the One with the "gentle and lowly" heart would be born here, registered in the house of David, of his lineage, to come forth as a ruler in Israel. He would come to be a shepherd who would rule in the strength of Yahweh, the I AM. And He will be our peace (Micah 5:4-5).

Observe the humility of our Jesus, born in a rural town, housed with the animals, bundled in a feeding trough, to a family unwelcome in their own relatives' homes in Bethlehem. The One who would rule came from lowly circumstances such as these.

Bethlehem means "house of bread" in Hebrew, and it was the very place that Naomi and Ruth returned after leaving Moab. It was in Bethlehem that Ruth gleaned wheat in Boaz's fields. Ruth and Boaz's son, Obed, was born there. His son, Jesse, followed, and then, of course, the shepherd-boy, David. David was anointed king in Bethlehem. It is no surprise that Jesus followed in his father David's footsteps: the Bread of Life, was born in the House of Bread. The Good Shepherd was adored by Bethlehem's own shepherds. The Son of David born in the City of David, to rule as king like His ancestor.

The coming of Jesus, in this way, to fulfill everything prophesied concerning Him, should cause us to fall on our knees in awe of the Great Conductor of this symphony of grace. God is always working in the small things, and in the seemingly insignificant places, to bring about His good purposes. Whatever small thing you put your hand to for Him today, remember He is working in you, both to will and to work for His good pleasure (Philippians 2:13). His attention to detail is praiseworthy! Thanks be to God for His indescribable gift!

* * *

Going Deeper

1. Do you feel small and insignificant in any area of life? Write them down.

2. How has God used you in the past to help others or to glorify Him?

3. Is there something you know you need to do, but you haven't done it because you think it won't matter, it's not important enough, or you're just plain scared? What is it?

4. Pray now and ask God for wisdom and direction with this step you feel you're supposed to take. Then write down three measurable steps you can take in the next few weeks to work toward that goal in faith.

CHAPTER 6: UNWELCOME

December 6

Perhaps your grandmother owned a nativity set, like mine did, complete with the holy family nestled snug and warm in the straw. Their clothes are colorful, their faces clean, and the scene conveys an environment of coziness and warmth. If only it was really like that! Historians believe Mary actually gave birth to Jesus in a cave—a cold, damp, smelly cave filled with livestock. Our Deliverer was delivered by a teenage mom unwelcome everywhere else.

> *And she gave birth to her firstborn son and wrapped him in swaddling cloths and laid him in a manger, because there was no place for them in the inn (Luke 2:7, ESV).*

When Joseph and Mary arrived in Bethlehem, it was highly likely they had family members who lived there since they were all from the tribe of Judah, specifically, the line of David. It would be more plausible that they would seek shelter with their family, in a guest room, rather than at an inn. If they did indeed go to an inn, it was because their family would not welcome them. Considering the scandal surrounding Mary's pregnancy, it isn't surprising they would be turned away from a guest room. The fact Bethlehem was overcrowded, due to the census registration, even being denied admittance to an inn isn't hard to believe; however, someone in Bethlehem offered a stable, perhaps a cave, where the livestock were housed. A manger became the bed of the Son of God.

It's disappointing to think that Jesus arrived, and so many missed it. Both Mary and Joseph had to walk by faith, trust the angels' messages, and make room for the Messiah in their own lives. Most residing in Bethlehem did not make room. Maybe they weren't looking in the first place.

We miss Him too, sometimes. Maybe we miss Him because we're too busy with our own plans and agendas to prepare Him room. Maybe we miss Him because we have no faith. Maybe we aren't looking?

O holy Child of Bethlehem,
descend to us, we pray,
Cast out our sin, and enter in,
be born in us today!

We hear the Christmas angels
the great glad tidings tell.
O come to us, abide with us,
our Lord Emmanuel.

FROM "O LITTLE TOWN OF BETHLEHEM" BY PHILLIPS BROOKS [1]

* * *

Going Deeper

1. Have you missed Him this Christmas season? Have your activities, shopping, and rushing around caused you to forget that Christmas is actually about Him?

2. Take some time to read the Christmas stories in Matthew 1 and Luke 1-2 and meditate on His coming.

3. Practically speaking, what would your next week

look like if you made space for Jesus?

CHAPTER 7: BORN IN THE LIKENESS OF MEN

December 7

His cry split that silent night. It wasn't laughter or a gentle coo; it was the cry of first breath. In taking on human form, Jesus entered the world the same way we all do, naked and wailing. The first cry accompanies the first breath, clears the lungs, and begins the process of involuntary breathing that continues until the day of death.

> *[W]ho, though he was in the form of God, did not count equality with God a thing to be grasped, but emptied himself, by taking the form of a servant, being born in the likeness of men (Philippians 2:6-7, ESV).*

He emptied Himself of His glory, left heaven, and came to earth to be a servant. The precious infant crying in the dark cave was God in the flesh, coming not to be served, but to serve. His cry commenced His mission.

> *And being found in human form, he humbled himself by becoming obedient to the point of death, even death on a cross (Philippians 2:8, ESV).*

His life ended the way it began: a beautiful symmetry marking the life of the Man of Sorrows. The naked Messiah let out a loud cry and breathed His last breath on the cross (Luke 23:46). Humble God came to earth in human form and died so that we might live. He was born naked and crying in a cave; He died, naked and crying, and was buried in a cave.

> *Therefore God has highly exalted him and bestowed on him the name that is above every name, so that at the name of Jesus every knee should bow, in heaven and on earth and under the earth, and every tongue confess that Jesus Christ is Lord, to the glory of God the Father (Philippians 2:9-11, ESV).*

The Holy Spirit, the *pneuma,* the breath of God, raised Him from the dead and exalted Him to His right hand. There He sits and waits for His second coming in which He will rule and reign as the king He is for all eternity. The cry that split the silent night over two thousand years ago cleared the way for a Servant God who would live, die, and rise to breathe that very same breath into our dead lungs and give us eternal life.

Silent Night, Holy Night,
Son of God, love's pure light.
Radiant beams from Thy holy face
With the dawn of redeeming grace.
Jesus, Lord, at Thy birth.
Jesus, Lord, at Thy birth.

FROM "SILENT NIGHT" BY
FATHER JOSEPH MOHR

* * *

Going Deeper

1. How has Jesus' life, death, and resurrection impacted your life?

2. How have you responded to His grace? Tears? Worship? Pushed it away?

3. What is a practical way you could “bow the knee” to Jesus today?

CHAPTER 8: EARS TO HEAR AND EYES TO SEE

December 8

The first group to hear the news of Jesus' birth were a group of rag-tag shepherds on the hills outside of Bethlehem. Our pastor, Matt Harris[1], shared with us one Sunday that shepherds were so disdained in the days of Jesus' birth that their testimony was considered unreliable in a court of law. How miraculous then is it that these are the people to whom God chose to speak—ones to whom society wouldn't believe or listen? He revealed His truth to the poor, the weak, the foolish, and the common. This is consistent with Jesus' own teaching in parables. When the disciples asked Him why He taught in parables, Jesus said,

This is why I speak to them in parables, because

seeing they do not see, and hearing they do not hear, nor do they understand...But blessed are your eyes, for they see, and your ears, for they hear. For truly, I say to you, many prophets and righteous people longed to see what you see, and did not see it, and to hear what you hear, and did not hear it (Matthew 13:13, 16-17, ESV).

God reveals Himself to those with hearing ears and seeing eyes.

The shepherds were such as these. In fact, their response to the message was not to hoard it for themselves or to elevate themselves over others for the revelation they received. What did they do?

And they went with haste and found Mary and Joseph, and the baby lying in a manger. And when they saw it, they made known the saying that had been told them concerning this child. And all who heard it wondered at what the shepherds told them...And the shepherds returned, glorifying and praising God for all they had heard and seen, as it had been told them (Luke 2:16-18,20, ESV).

Just as the faithful host in Hebrews 11 longed to see His day, and just as the shepherds saw it, we too can be recipients of the good tidings when we have eyes to see and ears to hear. Let us respond like the shepherds and rush to adore Him and proclaim His coming.

* * *

Going Deeper

1. Do you have eyes to see and ears to hear? How do you know?

2. If so, what are you doing with the good news? Are you sharing it with others?

3. Write out a prayer of praise and adoration for all

you've heard and seen concerning Jesus.

CHAPTER 9: MAGNIFICAT

December 9

Fig. 1 Remington, Sister Grace, Mary and Eve, 2003, pencil and crayon on paper, 11 x 14 in. Dubuque, Our Lady of the Mississippi Abbey. Reproduced with permission.

Two women, two stories, are connected from Genesis 3 to Luke 1 by a thread of redemption. In this drawing[1], Eve appears sorrowful, knowing that the fruit she carries represents that sinful rebellion and lack of faith in God's word to her. Mary, on the other hand, displays the mercy of God as she comforts Eve with the fruit of her womb, the seed that God promised would crush the head of the serpent, the same that entangled and deceived Eve.

I will put enmity between you and the woman,
and between your offspring and her offspring;
he shall bruise your head,
and you shall bruise his heel (Genesis 3:15, ESV).

Mary's foot stands on the serpent's head, vicariously crushing the serpent's head through giving birth to the Messiah. Jesus defeated the serpent by His death on the cross. We too live vicariously through Christ's death-blow to the serpent as we walk in the victory won for us on the cross. We are "more than conquerors through him who loved us" (Romans 8:37, ESV). Our position in Christ grants us authority over the evil one.

The juxtaposition of the two women—one called "the mother of all living," and the other, the mother of the living God-Man—shows us there is always redemption. Mary's faith in saying, "Let it be to me according to your word" (Luke 1:38, ESV), is contrasted with Eve's questioning of God's word to her in Eden. Where one failed to trust, the other succeeded, but this faith wasn't a result of Mary's own merit. In fact, the angel declared that she had found favor with God. That word for favor in Greek is "charis," meaning "grace." Mary found grace with God; she didn't earn it. It was a free gift of grace, given by God. The grace she received through Jesus is the same grace God offers us.

Will you, like Mary, receive His words and proclaim His magnificence as she did?

My soul magnifies the Lord,
and my spirit rejoices in God my Savior,
for he has looked on the humble estate of his servant.
For behold, from now on all generations will call me blessed;
for he who is mighty has done great things for me,
and holy is his name.
And his mercy is for those who fear him
from generation to generation

(Luke 1:46b-50, ESV).

* * *

Going Deeper

1. We've all been Eve, but not all have embraced the faith Mary lived. Where are you in your journey of faith? Are you still believing the lie that God is holding out on you, or do you see the grace and gift of Jesus He is extending to you?

2. Maybe you have walked the faith road for some time now. Do you recognize all is grace, unmerited favor, before God, and you can't earn His gift of love and redemption?

3. Take some time today to ask God to give you faith to trust Him and faith to realize that His gift of Jesus isn't based on how good you are or aren't. Embrace His grace today.

CHAPTER 10: THE BRANCH

December 10

A dead, lifeless stump was all that was left of the kingdoms of Israel and Judah after Assyria and Babylon had wrecked the landscape and carried off the inhabitants as slaves to their own countries. God had promised,

> *For thus says the LORD: David shall never lack a man to sit on the throne of the house of Israel (Jeremiah 33:17, ESV).*

All hope seemed lost. Where was the fulfillment of God's promise? The kingdom had split and fragmented following Solomon's death. King after king turned to idol worship. A few godly men rose up to tear down the high places, restore the worship of the one, true God in his temple, but the people continued to lust after foreign gods. In His divine fatherhood, God disciplined His people by removing them from the land He had promised them. It was prior to the Babylonian captivity that Isaiah received the following prophecies from the Lord.

There shall come forth a shoot from the stump of Jesse, and a branch from his roots shall bear fruit (Isaiah 11:1, ESV).

In that day the root of Jesse, who shall stand as a signal for the peoples—of him shall the nations inquire, and his resting place shall be glorious (Isaiah 11:10, ESV).

It would be nearly eight hundred years before this prophecy would be fulfilled in Jesus. He came forth from Judah's kingly line which had been laid bare like a felled tree, leaving only the stump behind. It was out of this brokenness that God sent Jesus as the Restorer of all things, the Promise sent in fulfillment of His word. Jesus is called both root of Jesse, and the branch from the root of Jesse! He is the Alpha and the Omega, the beginning and the end. He is everything!

Isaiah says,

For he grew up before him like a young plant,
and like a root out of dry ground;
he had no form or majesty that we should look at him,
and no beauty that we should desire him.
He was despised and rejected by men;

a man of sorrows, and acquainted with grief;
and as one from whom men hide their faces
he was despised, and we esteemed him not
(53:2-3, ESV).

He didn't come looking like a majestic king. He was rejected and despised. At the time of Jesus' birth, Herod, an Edomite king, was on the throne of Israel, more like a puppet ruler for the Romans than an actual monarch. He was not a descendent of David; he was an imposter filled with rage and jealousy when he heard from the wise men of another king being born. His jealousy led to a successful murder mission of all the baby boys under the age of two; however, it wasn't the end of Jesus' story.

Behold, the days are coming, declares the LORD, when I will raise up for David a righteous Branch, and he shall reign as king and deal wisely, and shall execute justice and righteousness in the land. In his days Judah will be saved, and Israel will dwell securely. And this is the name by which he will be called: 'The LORD is our righteousness' (Jerermiah 23:5-6, ESV).

The only way Jesus could be our righteousness was to first come as that Suffering Servant to put His righteousness on our account and pay the debt with His life. In this, He ushered in His Kingdom and will bring it to completion in His second coming. This is "good news of great joy that will be for all the people" (Luke 2:10, ESV).

* * *

Going Deeper

1. What seemingly dead dream or circumstance in your life looks as if it has no hope of growing?

2. Jesus didn't come looking the part of a king, and everyone was surprised how His life played out. Have you been surprised by Jesus and how He interacts in your life? How so?

3. Why is suffering often the gateway to growth? Have you seen this unfold in your own life?

4. Take some time to pray and ask God to give you Jesus' perspective on suffering and to be able to see His gentle hand leading you in it.

CHAPTER 11: CHILDREN BY FAITH

December 11

> *He took him outside and said, "Look up at the sky and count the stars—if indeed you can count them." Then he said to him, "So shall your offspring be." Abram believed the Lord, and he credited it to him as righteousness.*
>
> GENESIS 15:5-6, NIV

This promise of an heir in his old age seemed unthinkable, but offspring innumerable like the stars in the heavens? It would be nothing short of miraculous! Earlier God had promised him that He would bless him and make him a blessing and that ALL THE PEOPLES would be blessed through Abraham, the father of many nations (Genesis12:2-3). Isaac, Jacob, and Judah came. Many generations later, Jesse, David, and Solomon were born. How were ALL THE PEOPLES being blessed through Abraham? Surely not just the Jews?

One called "The Son of David" was born, Jesus, whose name means "God Saves." He was born of the tribe of Judah, and through His sinless life, His atoning death, and His victorious resurrection, ALL THE PEOPLES are blessed. When we, like Abraham, believe God, He credits our faith as righteousness (Romans 4:3-5). This is how God saves. Jesus comments on Abraham's faith in John 8:

> *"Your father Abraham rejoiced at the thought of seeing my day; he saw it and was glad."*
>
> *"You are not yet fifty years old," they said to him, "and you have seen Abraham!"*
>
> *"Very truly I tell you," Jesus answered, "before Abraham was born, I am!" (56-58, NIV).*

He was both before Abraham and the promised Seed of Abraham. The One who created the stars, who fashioned Abraham and his descendants in their mother's wombs, who credited Abraham's faith as righteousness, also grew in the womb of a descendant of Abraham in order to bless all the people of the world by crediting His own righteousness to each one who has faith in Him. This is amazing grace.

* * *

Going Deeper

1. Which promises of God have you found hard to believe?

2. How does Abraham's faith despite his circumstances encourage you to believe God?

3. Take a moment to worship Jesus for His eternal nature and His mind-boggling incarnation of God and Man in one person.

CHAPTER 12: TREASURING HIS PROMISES

December 12

The people of Bethlehem were in wonder at the news the shepherds exclaimed. How could this be? Was it true? The Christ is born?

But Mary treasured up all these things, pondering them in her heart (Luke 2:19, ESV).

She treasured up all these things: another glorious angelic appearance to some lowly shepherds out in a field nearby, a declaration that a Savior, a Son of David, the Messiah, had been born, not to her only, but to everyone—the shepherds, the town, and the world. Her son wasn't hers alone. She kept these truths close to her heart, safe and preserved, and

For to us a child is born,
to us a son is given;
and the government shall be upon his shoulder,
and his name shall be called
Wonderful Counselor, Mighty God,
Everlasting Father, Prince of Peace
(Isaiah 9:6, ESV).

* * *

Going Deeper

1. In what area of your life are you waiting for redemption? How is the coming of Jesus an answer to that waiting?

2. Make a list of the ways God has been faithful to

you this year. Share it with
like Anna, you can practice b
witness of His grace.

3. Maybe you haven't found the peace of God yet. Spend some time asking God to give you eyes to see Jesus as the Prince of Peace who can bring you peace with God and others. Ask Him to give you ears to hear Him calling you to follow Him.

CHAPTER 14: LISTENING FOR GOD

December 14

He'd been waiting, like the others. Though no prophetic books were written for four hundred years, God had not been silent to Simeon.

Now there was a man in Jerusalem, whose name was Simeon, and this man was righteous and devout, waiting for the consolation of Israel, and the Holy Spirit was upon him. And it had been revealed to him by the Holy Spirit that he would not see death before he had seen the Lord's Christ (Luke 2:25-26, ESV).

He knew he would meet the Messiah, the consolation, or comfort, of Israel, before his death. Perhaps this was not a true four hundred years of silence. God kept revealing and faithfully kept His word to Simeon.

> *And he came in the Spirit into the temple, and when the parents brought in the child Jesus, to do for him according to the custom of the Law, he took him up in his arms and blessed God and said, "Lord, now you are letting your servant depart in peace, according to your word; for my eyes have seen your salvation that you have prepared in the presence of all peoples, a light for revelation to the Gentiles, and for glory to your people Israel" (Luke 2:27-32, ESV).*

What would it have been like to know that the Deliverer has arrived for *all* the people? God is a global God. He chose Israel to be a blessing to the world through the Messiah Jesus. Simeon knew this, because God "does nothing without revealing his secret to his servants the prophets" (Amos 3:7, ESV).

His revelation didn't stop with Simeon. Through Simeon, He spoke to Mary, explaining Jesus' role on the earth,

> *Behold, this child is appointed for the fall and rising of many in Israel, and for a sign that is opposed (and a sword will pierce through your own soul also), so that thoughts from many hearts may be revealed (Luke 2:34-35, ESV).*

The word of God is sharp; it pierces. Jesus came to expose our hearts so we could draw near to His throne of grace (Heb. 4:12-16, ESV). Grant us ears to hear, Lord, and faith to believe Your word.

* * *

Going Deeper

1. Have there been times in your life when you felt like God was silent? What did you do in those times?

2. How has God revealed Himself to you?

3. What are some practical ways you can reveal Jesus to others?

CHAPTER 15: THE GLORY OF THE LORD HAS COME

December 15

What if that Star of Bethlehem wasn't a conglomeration of planets and stars aligned as some suppose? What if instead, like so many other elements of the story of Jesus' birth, it was a miracle? Lasting up to two years, this star came to rest over the place where Jesus lived, heralding the arrival of the King of Kings. What if the starlight in the sky was the glory of God rising over the infant Jesus, the true Light of the world?

Arise, shine, for your light has come,
and the glory of the LORD has risen upon you.
For behold, darkness shall cover the earth,
and thick darkness the peoples;

but the LORD will arise upon you,
and his glory will be seen upon you.
And nations shall come to your light,
and kings to the brightness of your rising...
They shall bring gold and frankincense,
and shall bring good news, the praises of the LORD (Isaiah 60:1-3,6b, ESV).

Jesus ushered in the glory of the Lord, bringing heaven to earth. Men from other nations came to worship Him to fulfill these words prophesied seven hundred years prior. What glory!!

The heavens declare the glory of God,
and the sky above proclaims his handiwork (Psalm 19:1, ESV).

His creation declares His praise and glory in the earth. His light shines in our darkness, so that He may increase our joy in Him and heal the wounds caused by sin. We need only to turn our faces to the Light.

The people who walked in darkness
have seen a great light;
those who dwelt in a land of deep darkness,
on them has light shone.
You have multiplied the nation;
you have increased its joy (Isaiah 9:2-3a, ESV).

Have you seen the Light? Do you rejoice, and like the star, proclaim the glory of the Lord?

> *You are the light of the world. A city set on a hill cannot be hidden...let your light shine before others, so that they may see your good works and give glory to your Father who is in heaven (Matthew 5:14,16, ESV).*

This glory of God just keeps echoing from heaven to earth and back again.

* * *

Going Deeper

1. What is the glory of God?

2. How does His glory impact you personally?

3. What would it look like for you to declare His glory in your sphere of influence?

CHAPTER 16: GIFTS FOR JESUS

December 16

There are myriad mysteries surrounding the identities and homeland of the wise men who came to worship the Christ child. Experts agree that we don't know how many there actually were, we don't know if they rode horses or camels (or both!), and we don't know how many gifts of gold, frankincense, and myrrh they brought along. But what we do know is that their arrival was prophesied in Isaiah, and it seems to be a double prophecy, made both for the first and second comings of Jesus!

> *And nations shall come to your light,*
> *and kings to the brightness of your rising...*
> *the wealth of the nations shall come to you.*
> *A multitude of camels shall cover you,*
> *the young camels of Midian and Ephah;*
> *all those from Sheba shall come.*

They shall bring gold and frankincense,
and shall bring good news, the praises of the LORD
(Isaiah 60:3,5b-6, ESV).

It is astonishing that the purpose of the wise men's visit was worship. They told Herod that they wondered at His location because they had come to worship Him (Matthew 2:2). Ambassadors from countries would often bring gifts of tribute to great kings, just as the Queen of Sheba brought her entourage to King Solomon's court, bearing gifts. And while these men likely came from that same region of Sheba, they didn't just come to bring tribute and to show mutual respect; they came to bow down, to recognize His authority and rule.

And going into the house they saw the child with Mary his mother, and they fell down and worshipped Him. Then, opening their treasures, they offered Him gifts, gold and frankincense and myrrh (Matthew 2:11, ESV).

May our hearts kneel before Him each day, offering Him our treasures, because we, like the wise men, bring "good news, the praises of the Lord" to others (Isaiah 60:6b, ESV).

He rules the world with truth and grace,
And makes the nations prove
The glories of His righteousness

And wonders of His love,
And wonders of His love,
And wonders, wonders of His love.

FROM "JOY TO THE WORLD" BY
ISAAC WATTS[1]

* * *

Going Deeper

1. What gifts do you have to offer Jesus this Christmas? Your money? Your time? Your attention?

2. How can you worship Him wholeheartedly this season?

3. How does worshiping Jesus and giving Him your gifts cause your mouth to overflow with His praises?

CHAPTER 17: TOPPLING THRONES

December 17

We're told both in historical documents and the Bible that King Herod was a bloody, ruthless king. He was such a monster he ordered the murder of all baby boys under the age of two in hopes of destroying the baby king the wise men had come to worship. What was the motive behind such an act?

Herod was worried that the kingdom he'd built himself was about to crumble because a baby had been born. He knew the prophecies. He didn't doubt what the wise men told him about the star they saw and their desire to come worship this new king. Fear of losing his kingdom pushed Herod to commit this wicked massacre of babies and toddlers. It's a disgusting display of greed, selfishness, and pride, and we mourn the unimaginable loss of so many precious lives.

Lest we think we are better than Herod, we must ask the question of ourselves: what kinds of sins do we commit in order to preserve the kingdom we've built for ourselves? Don't we all want to be worshiped? Don't we expect others to put us first? Our egos swell when people praise or flatter us. In our flesh, we desire worship. Maybe we've expected praise for a job well done, but we were overlooked. A sense of entitlement rises up in our hearts, and then we're angry—because we deserve more, but really because the legs on our thrones are shaking. Our kingdoms of self are built on the shifting sand of human ego. We worship ourselves, and we expect everyone else to follow suit—to meet our needs, to praise us, to bow to our wishes and desires, and we're willing to do whatever it takes to keep that throne from tottering.

We, like Herod, need Jesus to set us free from these shaky, crumbly sandcastle kingdoms we've constructed. In contrast, His kingdom will never end, and when we fall at His feet in worship, we find He is enough for us. Only He brings us ultimate fulfillment and happiness.

* * *

Going Deeper

1. What does your sandcastle kingdom seek after most?

2. Are there times where you expect others to bow to you? Your spouse? Your kids? Family or friends? What does that look like?

3. When one kingdom conquers another, the defeated kingdom surrenders and comes into submission of the new king. What does surrender to King Jesus look like for you today?

CHAPTER 18: WHO IS THIS KING OF GLORY?

December 18

Shortly after the wise men departed, Joseph had a dream in which the angel of the Lord told him,

> *Rise, take the child and his mother, and flee to Egypt, and remain there until I tell you, for Herod is about to search for the child, to destroy him (Matthew 2:13, ESV).*

So Joseph took them in the middle of the night and went to Egypt to fulfill what the prophet Hosea had prophesied, "[O]ut of Egypt I called my son" (11:1, ESV).

Moses, whose name means "drawn out," was hidden in the Nile as a baby as well as in the wilderness from the Pharaoh who sought his life. God hid Moses for 40 years before He used him to save and draw His people out of Egyptian slavery. Similarly, Jesus, "God Saves," was hidden in Egypt from Herod who sought His life. God hid Jesus in Egypt for a few years and then in the no-name town of Nazareth until His thirtieth year. It was at that time He began His public ministry to draw His own people out of slavery and bring the ultimate deliverance to the world.

God's plan from the beginning was deliverance. His plan to set us free from the slavery of sin and the dominion of death, the grave, and the works of the devil, was prophesied over and over. From Genesis 3:15, in which He promised a Seed who would crush the head of the serpent, to Malachi 3:1, in which He promised the coming of the Lord to His temple, God's rescue plan was revealed. His plan was not thwarted, though it was opposed; it was not prevented, though the enemies of God revolted.

No, Jesus came! He came, lived, died, rose, and He reigns victoriously over every enemy of God. God's plan has come to fruition, friends, and it's not over yet. He will come again and receive us unto Himself. Then we shall always be with the Lord.

Lift up your heads, O gates!
And lift them up, O ancient doors,
that the King of glory may come in.
Who is this King of glory?
The LORD of hosts,

he is the King of glory! (Psalm 24:9-10, ESV).

* * *

Going Deeper

1. Take a moment and worship the King of glory. Praise Him for all He's done, and all He will do.

2. How has Jesus delivered you in the past? Thank Him now.

3. Maybe there's a situation or a sin that you're struggling with, and you need deliverance? Cry out to Him now. He will deliver; He will save.

CHAPTER 19: ANGELIC CURIOSITY

December 19

They're everywhere in the Christmas story. They appear face to face with Zechariah and Mary. A multitude of them light up the sky to the shepherds outside of Bethlehem. They appear in dreams to Joseph three times, and possibly once to the wise men.

Angels—ministers of God, messengers, ministers of flaming fire—live in the presence of God, behold His face, carry His messages, and proclaim His glory. Over the years, cultures have revered them, even worshiped them. They have been portrayed as beautiful women, as strong, muscular men, and even as chubby babies. People are fascinated by their power, their protection, and their other-worldliness. Ironically, these magnificent creatures are fascinated by how the gospel is prophesied to humans.

> *It was revealed to them [the prophets] that they were serving not themselves but you, in the things that have now been announced to you through those who preached the good news to you by the Holy Spirit sent from heaven, things into which angels long to look (1 Peter 1:12, ESV).*

Angels have declared His message, but it's not entirely clear to them. They rejoice when one sinner repents, but their longing is to understand this grace God has bestowed on His people. Isn't it kind of strange? Maybe it's because there is no redemption for their kind. Those that fell with Lucifer will remain separated from the King of Kings. The salvation of humankind intrigues them.

Humans may be distracted by the glory of angels and the power that God has given them, but angels, more rightly, are fascinated by the Gospel—that God would love humankind with such a radical display through the death, burial, and resurrection of His Son, Jesus. The Gospel is captivating; it is good tidings, great joy for all. It is peace with God; it solves every problem and unites us with the God who loves us. Even angels long to look into these things. Do you?

❋ ❋ ❋

Going Deeper

1. Do you still feel the "thrill of hope" when you hear the Gospel? Does it still excite you, or has it become commonplace?

2. Spend some time today meditating on Romans 8:31-39.

3. Describe God's great love for you in Jesus using words from the passage above.

CHAPTER 20: PREPARE THE WAY

December 20

The announcement concerning John's impending birth was mysterious and caused many people to wonder who he would be. Zechariah, who initially did not have faith his son would be born, was later filled with the Holy Spirit and prophesied over his son:

> *And you, child, will be called prophet of the Most High; for you will go before the Lord to prepare his ways, to give knowledge of salvation to his people, in the forgiveness of their sins (Luke 1:76-77, ESV).*

John grew into a wild man, living in the wilderness, feasting on locusts and honey, wearing animal skins, and stunning the people as he called for a baptism of repentance for the forgiveness of sins. Some were confused; they thought maybe John was the Messiah, but John set them straight:

> *I baptize you with water, but he who is mightier than I is coming, the strap of whose sandals I am not worthy to untie. He will baptize you with the Holy Spirit and with fire (Luke 3:16, ESV).*

The Apostle John, disciple of Jesus, says this of John the Baptist,

> *He came as a witness, to bear witness about the light, that all might believe through him (John 1:7, ESV).*

John's job was no different than yours or mine. Our calling is to prepare the way for Jesus—to announce His coming, to call people to repent and be forgiven of their sins, to humble ourselves and decrease so that He may increase. John was the forerunner of Jesus' first coming. We are the forerunners of His second coming. Let us proclaim His salvation. Let us stun the people with news of His arrival and future return.

For Elijah's voice is crying
In the desert far and near,
Bidding all men to repentance,
Since the kingdom now is here.

Oh that warning cry obey,
Now prepare for God a way;
Let the valleys rise to meet Him,
And all the hills bow down to greet Him."

FROM "COMFORT, COMFORT, YE MY PEOPLE" BY JOHANN OLEARIUS[1]

* * *

Going Deeper

1. What are you saying, doing, or showing to prepare the way of Jesus?

2. In your sphere of influence, are you willing to decrease so that He may increase? What would that look like?

3. Ask Him now for wisdom to see the places you can

herald His arrival and future return.

CHAPTER 21: THE WEIGHT OF THE WORLD

December 21

We all carry burdens, some of our own making, some on behalf of others, and some that we've picked up via legalistic beliefs. Jesus entered the world at a burdensome time. His people were under Roman occupation, not free to do as they pleased. The religious leaders of the day had lists a mile long of laws to follow to keep from breaking the actual Law God had given. Many were crushed under the weight of poverty and illness. And this is the world He came into on that starlit night over two thousand years ago.

His cousin John ran ahead of Him, figuratively speaking, announcing His arrival. John was then thrown into prison, awaiting his own death. John sent his disciples to Jesus to ask if He was really the One for whom they'd been waiting. Jesus doesn't condemn John's question; in fact, He praises him more highly than any other human and reassures John's disciples that He is fulfilling the prophecies of setting captives free, healing blind eyes, and making the lame walk. He really had come to show a different way. He condemns those cities who didn't repent despite these wonderful signs of His arrival, and then He turns to those around Him and invites them to come to Him. He sees their childlike faith and the burdens they've borne and promises rest for their souls.

> *Come to Me, all who labor and are heavy laden, and I will give you rest. Take my yoke upon you, and learn from me, for I am gentle and lowly in heart, and you will find rest for your souls. For my yoke is easy, and my burden is light (Matthew 11:28-30, ESV).*

Maybe this Christmas you're feeling like it's all too much to carry. His invitation is open to you—come to Him. Nothing is too heavy when Jesus is beside you. Lean into His frame, knowing He bore the cross for you, and whatever cross you bear daily, you won't carry it alone.

The King of kings lay thus in lowly manger,
In all our trials born to be our Friend.
He knows our need—to our weakness
is no stranger

Behold your King; before Him lowly bend
Behold your King; before Him lowly bend"

FROM "O HOLY NIGHT" BY
PLACIDE CAPPEAU

* * *

Going Deeper

1. Are you overwhelmed by the burdens in your life? What are they? List them here.

2. How would you categorize those burdens you just listed? Are there any that you've put on yourself that aren't actually necessary? Are you carrying the weight of unreasonable expectations from yourself or others? Are there any that you're carrying in order to gain favor with God? Think through those, releasing them in prayer to Jesus.

3. What would it look like for you to come to Jesus and learn rest from Him today?

CHAPTER 22: WHAT CHILD IS THIS?

December 22

The Pharisees in their self-righteousness couldn't fathom that Jesus was actually telling the truth about where He came from. How could He be as righteous as they? In what is one of the most intense passages of Scripture, they go so far as to insinuate Jesus was an illegitimately born child.

> *We were not born of sexual immorality. We have one Father—even God (John 8:41, ESV).*

He likely had heard the whispers and accusations His whole life—how Joseph wasn't His biological father, just the poor dope who got hornswoggled into marrying a promiscuous girl. But He's unruffled by their comments because His identity was secure:

> *If God were your Father, you would love me, for I came from God and I am here. I came not of my own accord, but he sent me (John 8:42, ESV).*

Scandal marked His birth, and even His adoptive father, Joseph, had wondered about Mary. But God revealed His plan to Joseph in a dream, and he didn't hesitate to take her as his wife. And in this great step of faith, Joseph was accepting the accusations as well as the responsibility of raising a child not from his own body. We don't hear anything about Joseph after Jesus was twelve years old, but his place in this story is worth honoring. His faith to obey God and walk a hard road, to lose his reputation, certainly sets an example for all of us who follow Jesus. Jesus, like Joseph, "made himself of no reputation, and took upon him the form of a servant" (Philippians 2:7, KJV).

There's no denying that the Christian life is a hard road: a road of no reputation, a road of assuming the form of a servant. We can surrender our reputation because our identity is secure—we are children of God and servants of God. "What Child is this?" We can say with Joseph, "He is mine."

* * *

Going Deeper

1. In what arenas of your life have you been concerned about your image or reputation?

2. Do you find yourself tying your identity to what you do? To who your family is? To your place in society? List ways you've done that here.

3. If you root yourself in your identity as a child of God, how does that affect your perspective when people don't approve of you? When people don't ap-

plaud you? When people don't recognize you or the work you've done?

4. Take some time to offer this up to the Father and ask Him to give you eyes to see yourself like He does and to be able to operate out of that true identity. He is yours, and you are His.

CHAPTER 23: GOD WITH US

December 23

The world is full of tragedy. Families daily lose children, spouses, and parents to illness and accidents, and the weight of death hangs like a heavy fog in the wintry morning sky.

There's a lot of talk about Heaven and the hope of going there to be reunited with the ones we love. As I've continued reading Scripture, I've noticed the focus for the believer is rarely on "going to heaven" and more on the resurrection of our actual bodies. And I have asked myself, "What's the difference? Isn't it just semantics? Heaven? Resurrection? I know what people mean when they say it, but isn't there something more to eternity than life as a disembodied spirit in Heaven?"

There is. It's interesting that Paul stresses in Colossians that the fullness of God dwells in Jesus' actual body (2:9). Jesus is truly the Son of God; heaven came to earth in a BODY. And when we see Jesus, in His bodily form (which He still has), we see the fullness of God. He goes on to say that we have been filled IN

HIM. Whatever happened to Jesus has happened to us—we have died, have been spiritually raised, will be physically raised and our bodies transformed into a body like His (1 Corinthians 15:42-49).

We humans dwell in corruptible bodies. One day, those of us in Christ will be physically resurrected, and our bodies as they are now (whether dead or alive) will be transformed into incorruptible bodies (1 Corinthians 15:52-55). We will live forever on the new earth where God Himself, with the new heaven, will come to dwell with us, just as Jesus came to dwell among us the first time.

> *Then I saw a new heaven and a new earth, for the first heaven and the first earth had passed away, and the sea was no more. And I saw the holy city, new Jerusalem, coming down out of heaven from God, prepared as a bride adorned for her husband. And I heard a loud voice from the throne saying, "Behold, the dwelling place of God is with man. He will dwell with them, and they will be his people, and God himself will be with them as their God" (Revelation 21:1-3, ESV).*

Heaven came to earth in the form of Jesus over two thousand years ago, and make no mistake about it, He is coming to earth again to establish the fullness of His kingdom here. We were made for this planet. We were given bodies, and while heaven currently is paradise and a temporary dwelling place for the disembodied believers, someday, He will renew it all—

heaven, earth, and these bodies (which will be fit for both heaven and earth!), so that we will always be together with the Lord. That is the greater hope: full restoration of our full personhood (body and spirit) in perfect communion with the God of the universe who always comes to dwell with us.

Even so, come Lord Jesus.

* * *

Going Deeper

1. What griefs have you carried this year? List them.

2. How does the resurrection give you hope for those griefs?

3. What ways have you seen God redeem situations, relationships, or sinful struggles in your life?

CHAPTER 24: BORN TO DIE

December 24

No more let sins and sorrows grow,
Nor thorns infest the ground;
He comes to make his blessings flow
Far as the curse is found.

FROM "JOY TO THE WORLD" BY ISAAC WATTS[1]

Do you feel the weight of sin and strife in your relationships? In our culture? On the world's stage? Christmas is ultimately about redemption, and Advent is waiting for the Redeemer to come. Galatians 3:13-14 (ESV) says,

> *Christ redeemed us from the curse of the law by becoming a curse for us—for it is written, "Cursed is everyone who is hanged on a tree"—so that in Christ Jesus the blessing of Abraham might come to the Gentiles, so that we might receive the promised*

Spirit through faith.

Sin and strife still mark our days more than we like to admit. There are conflicts, fits of anger, revenge, dissension, fighting, and accusations flying around like arrows shot straight from our tongues. There are thorns, the cares of this world and the deceitfulness of riches, that choke out the word that has been sown. We are all desperate for a Savior and King to repair the brokenness.

Aren't you grateful for Jesus? He came to make His blessings flow! He became the curse for us so that we Gentiles could also receive His blessing and be joined to Him in the Spirit. He declares in John 12:32 (ESV),

> *And I, when I am lifted up from the earth, will draw all people to myself.*

The Son of God was born to die, born to rise. This is Good News, friends! Receive this blessing by faith: He became a curse on your behalf to redeem you, to redeem this earth, and to rule over it all with truth and grace.

❋ ❋ ❋

Going Deeper

1. What strife-laden weight are you carrying today?

2. How does hope in Jesus help you cast off that strife and division?

3. How does faith in God's truth found in Galatians 5:16-26 set you free from strife?

CHAPTER 25: THE WEARY WORLD *STILL* REJOICES!

December 25

God came in the flesh. He is Immanuel, God with us. The story began with God walking in the cool of the day in a garden with the crown of His creation, humankind. Sin entered the world, but He didn't stay away.

He came again and again to be with His people. He came to meet with Abraham and promise him a son. He came down to the mountain to meet with Moses. He came to encourage Joshua in the battle. He came to the three Hebrews in the fiery furnace; however, in all those instances, He came in a pre-incarnate form, not in a body. But now, He has come to us as a baby, in the flesh, God incarnate.

He is the Word of God. He is the information about who God is, wrapped up in a body like ours. He is acquainted with all our ways, our temptations, and our griefs. He is not overcome by them. He is filled with all the fullness of God, full of grace and truth.

He is the I AM, the all-fulfilling One, who is pleased to dwell in Jesus. His pleasure to be at home with us, to make His dwelling among humankind, is soul-altering. No wonder the shepherds eagerly bowed before this babe! No wonder wise men sought Him out!

His authority stands against all the emptiness of human philosophy and tradition. Jesus was sent in the flesh to condemn sin in the flesh and fulfill the righteous requirement of the Law in us, who walk according to the Spirit! This is amazing grace and truth lived out by our Lord Jesus. The future is bright: the dwelling place of God will be with humankind, forever and ever. The weary world *still* rejoices!

O holy night! The stars are brightly shining;
It is the night of our dear Savior's birth.
Long lay the world in sin and error pining,
'Til He appeared and the soul felt its worth.

A thrill of hope—the weary world rejoices,
For yonder breaks a new and glorious morn!

Fall on your knees! O hear the angel voices!
O night divine, O night when
Christ was born!

O night, O holy night, O night divine!

FROM "O HOLY NIGHT" BY
PLACIDE CAPPEAU

* * *

Going Deeper

1. How does it feel to know that Jesus understands your struggles, temptations, and sorrows because He, too, walked this planet in a body like yours?

2. How do you react when you feel like you're alone? Where do you run?

3. What would it look like for you to embrace the love

of Jesus this Christmas season and find your belonging in Him?

NOTES

Chapter 4: God's Faithfulness in the Journey

1. Brooks, Phillips. Lyrics to "O Little Town of Bethlehem." Hymnary.org, 2007. https://hymnary.org/text/o_little_town_of_bethlehem.

Chapter 6: Unwelcome

1. Brooks, Phillips. Lyrics to "O Little Town of Bethlehem." Hymnary.org, 2007. https://hymnary.org/text/o_little_town_of_bethlehem.

Chapter 7: Born in the Likeness of Men

1. Mohr, Father Joseph. Lyrics to "Silent Night, Holy Night." *Hymnary.org*, 2007. https://hymnary.org/text/silent_night_holy_night_all_is_calm_all.

Chapter 8: Ears to Hear and Eyes to See

1. Harris, Matt. Sunday Morning Service, Eagle Creek Church, 13 December 2020, Lee's Summit, Missouri. Sermon.

This sermon can be viewed here: https://www.youtube.com/watch?v=MdFHLAoz7sI

Chapter 9: Magnificat

1. Remington, Sister Grace. Mary and Eve. 2003. Our Lady of the Mississippi Abbey. Monastery Candy. Our Lady of the Mississippi Abbey. Web. 19 October 2021.

Chapter 13: Waiting for Redemption

1. Longfellow, Henry Wadsworth. "Christmas Bells." *Favorite Poems Old and New*, edited by Helen Ferris, Doubleday and Company, Inc., 1957, 85-86.

Chapter 16: Gifts for Jesus

1. Watts, Isaac. Lyrics to "Joy to the World." Hymnary.org, 2007. https://hymnary.org/text/joy_to_the_world_the_lord_is_come.

Chapter 20: Prepare the Way

1. Olearius, Johannes. Lyrics to "Comfort, Comfort Ye My People." Hymnary.org, 2007. https://hymnary.org/hymn/ELH91895/a119

Chapter 21: The Weight of the World

1. Cappeau, Placide. Lyrics to "Oh Holy Night." Hymnary.org, 2007. https://hymnary.org/text/o_holy_night_the_stars_are_brightly_shin

Chapter 24: Born to Die

1. Watts, Isaac. Lyrics to "Joy to the World." Hymnary.org, 2007. https://hymnary.org/text/joy_to_the_world_the_lord_is_come.

Chapter 25: The Weary World Still Rejoices!

1. Cappeau, Placide. Lyrics to "Oh Holy Night." Hymnary.org, 2007. https://hymnary.org/text/o_holy_night_the_stars_are_brightly_shin

ACKNOWLEDGEMENTS

Jesus, this book is for You. I want You to be glorified in my writing. Thank You for life, breath, ideas, and amazing grace. Thank You for being with me.

Dave, you're my dream come true. The way you love and support me, give me the freedom to chase my dreams, and buy me Hy-vee drinks is a constant reminder of your love. Thanks for encouraging me to keep going and for following Jesus as you lead us in our family adventures.

Sam, Maryn, Lucy, Felix, Milo, and Leif, you're my symphony, my gift to the world, and I'm so proud to be your mom. I can't wait to see the adventures Jesus takes you on as you grow older. Thank you for all the grace to spend some time writing and for forgiving me when I mess up. Thank you, specifically, to Maryn who helped bring the cover design and all the social media images to completion. Your tippy-tap skills and eye for beauty helped so much!

Mom and Dad, thank you for giving me Jesus. He was the best gift you could give, and you were faithful to keep me where I would hear about Him all the time. I can't thank you enough.

Anna, I really couldn't do this without your cheerleading and advice. Thank you for all the messages, the laughter, the prayers, and for always pushing me to KEEP GOING. You have been a fantastic, long-distance friend, and I look forward to the new earth where we will live down the street from one another.

Lindsey, I know it was the providence of God that we reconnected after nearly 20 years of not seeing each other. I am so grateful to have found you again, and in so doing, found you still faithful to Jesus and sharing Him with others. Thank you for editing this book and for being committed to me as a friend. My thanks pale in comparison to the gift you are to me.

Gina, you have been a delightful and encouraging surprise in my story. I am so grateful we connected last year, and I'm thankful for your friendship, your encouragement, and your wisdom. Thank you for editing this manuscript and showing your love in this very tangible way. I'm looking forward to our next cup of tea.

Kate, you had no idea that day if I would pick up that bookmark or not, but you painted it anyway in faith. I'm grateful you're a part of this story, and I'm so honored to have your art on the cover. I love how God has made you and gifted you to love on His people and minister to their hearts. This collaboration has given me so much joy.

Nicole, our conversations have been the fuel for so much writing. I'm so glad we're here now, just down the street from y'all. Thank you for going deep, for listening, and for being exactly who you are. Thank you for believing in me and always pushing me forward.

Madi, your offer to take things off my plate was a gift. One less thing to think about in this process was exactly what I needed. I'm excited to see how God is going to complete the work He started in you. You're His.

I'm so grateful to my launch team for helping me get the word out about this book. Every share and every review is a gift, and I'm so thankful y'all showed up and supported me. I hope you were blessed in the process as you shared, knowing that you weren't just sharing my book—you were sharing Jesus.

Eagle Creek Church, Matt, Sheri, and everyone else, thank you for encouraging me to be who God made me to be. Your love, faith, and encouragement helped me to step out.

And you, reader, who bought this book or received it as a gift, thank you for reading. I pray you're blessed with a deeper knowledge of Christ, His love, and His grace toward you.

ABOUT THE AUTHOR

Amanda Geidl

is a friend of God, a wife to Dave, and a mother to six wonderful children between the ages of 6-16. She has been writing for years, in between having babies, homeschooling, and ministering to women, both in the USA and in Asia. She enjoys reading books, cooking delicious food, watching the Kansas City Chiefs, and trying to make her dogs snuggle her. She currently lives in the Kansas City metro area.

Website: amandageidl.com
Facebook: @amandageidl
Instagram: @amandageidl
Email: amanda@amandageidl.com

ABOUT THE ARTIST

Kate Ranstrom is an artist who has always loved color and using a variety of media for her art. Through the past several years as a stay-at-home mom of three, she felt called by the Lord to paint for His purposes. She was first asked to paint in the healing rooms at her church where she ministered to the sick through her paintings. Since stepping out during that season, the Lord has led her to minister to many individuals through her prayer art.

Kate designed and painted the cover for this book. She used acrylic paint and ink on canvas and her own beautiful imagination.

You can check out more of her work, purchase art cards and prints, or order a personal art piece at her website below.

Website: Heaventoearthart.net
Facebook: @HeavenToEarthArt
Email: KateRanstrom@yahoo.com

Made in the USA
Coppell, TX
21 November 2022

86796525R00063